TEACHING POETRY TO CHILDREN

by

David Greenberg

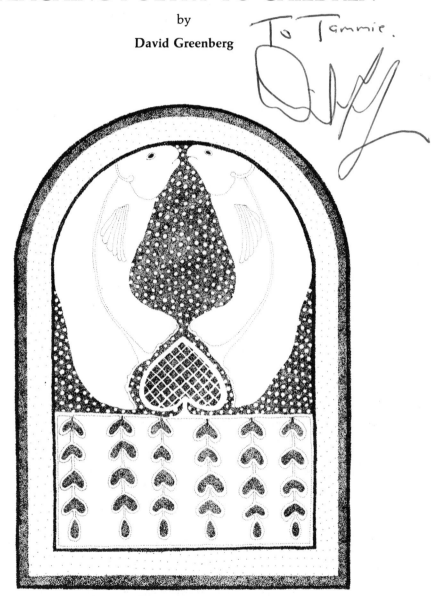

Illustrations by Diane Vanderpool

David Greenberg is a poet who conducts poetry-readings, childrens' writing workshops, and teachers' workshops. He has taught mountaineering, worked nightshifts in a tavern, and run his own eggroll restaurant. He now devotes his principal energies to writing and teaching poetry to students and teachers. David also appears on TV and radio.

This poetry-teaching manual has been developed after thousands of hours of experience working with teachers and students of all ages.

David Greenberg can be reached for poetry readings and workshops by contacting Continuing Education Publications.

Preface

Many of my ideas are unconventional, for I am concerned with content in poetry, not form. I am concerned with poetry which genuinely touches a student's imagination and feelings. I am anti-nursery rhyme. I am anti-pedantry. The ideas I present here work; they have proven themselves with thousands of students.

READ WITH AN OPEN MIND!

Table of Contents

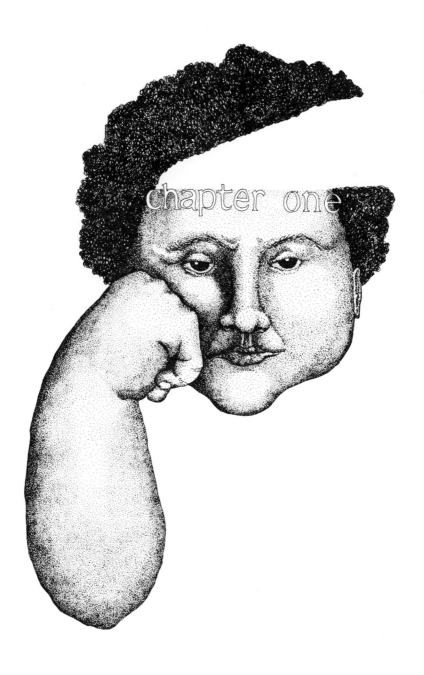

chapter one

Ways Not To Teach Poetry

Most people don't like poetry. They find it either boring or incomprehensible, and usually both. Considering the way poetry typically is taught, this is quite understandable. Haven't you ever had a teacher read you a poem and then ask you (in what I always recall as a faintly ominous tone) "What is the deep meaning of this poem?" And then the poem turns into a torturous puzzle—for it seems that whenever one "deep meaning" is found, there's always another beneath it. And always the deep meaning you find is never quite the same as the one the poet (or teacher) intended.

It is critical when teaching children or beginners poetry to remember GUIDELINE ONE: Do not ask students to figure out the deep meaning of poems. For most people this is the equivalent, in enjoyment ar.d learning, to deciphering Russian cryptograms. This is not to deny that meaning is an important part of poetry. But poetry has *many* facets that can be appreciated, and meaning or deep understanding is one that takes many years of living experience to appreciate. Perhaps you'll have a young student who is remarkably insightful. In that case break Guideline One.

Another destructive way in which poetry is taught is what I call the mechanical approach. The poetry unit is started by breaking poetry down into its "essential" parts: rhyme, meter, alliteration, onomatopoeia, metaphor, simile, scansion, branks, and galantines. First, I must confess here, that though I am recognized by some as a poet, I still am not quite certain what an iambic-pentameter is. And I'm positive that this uncertainty has made no difference in the quality of my poetry. Poetry is no more iambic pentameter + metaphor than art is paint + canvas. And even if you do not agree with this analogy, I will flatly state that almost all children find the mechanical approach boring, and that is reason enough not to teach it.

Children, especially, seem to think of poetry as rhyme. For

3

instance, the following is a typical example of a child's poem.

> *Once I had a* spoon
> *It was in the month of* June
> *And suddenly I heard a* tune
> *Of a* raccoon
> *But no it was only a* balloon

This is a pretty lousy poem. Probably you've read a good deal of cute poetry just like it. The reason it's poor is that the rhyme in the poem almost entirely precludes a whole range of other possible poetic qualities. After all, how can a student be expected to voice a sense of imaginative beauty or depth of feeling when the primary concern is finding a word which will rhyme with "spoon." This chore is made even more difficult by the child's smaller vocabulary. Perhaps it is all the early *Mother Goose* and Dick and Jane reading primers that teach this concept of poetry. Anyway, stay away from the mechanical approach, and . . . **GUIDELINE TWO: When teaching poetry, always state explicitly that you do not want any rhyming.** Perhaps at a later point mechanics and rhyme might be valuable, but not in the beginning stages.

Also, (need I mention it?) an unfortunate technique widely used for teaching poetry is memorization. It's major fault, again, is that for most young people it's boring. Thus, **GUIDELINE THREE: Never force your students to memorize poetry.**

chapter two

What is Poetry?

A good question at this point is "What is poetry?" That's difficult to answer because poetry means so many different things to different people. Here is the best I can do: POETRY IS PRESSURIZED LANGUAGE. Poetry is language which really hits — language which we more than passively register, language which is evocative, language which stirs laughter or thought or fears or inexplicable feelings in ourselves.

We live with language; indeed there are those who say that reality is nothing but language. Yet it is so natural to us, so omnipresent, that we are hardly cognizant of it, probably in the same way that a fish is hardly cognizant of water. For instance, have you ever paid attention to the sounds of language? Many of the most normal words have bizarrely beautiful sounds. Yet, just like the wrappers on candy bars, we quickly and unappreciatively discard sounds to get at what's inside, i.e. their meaning. Try a little experiment. Just imagine that you have never heard anyone speak and you walk up to someone who says suddenly the word "b-e-l-l-y-b-u-t-t-o-n." Aside from this being a very strange introduction, just listen to the sound of this word. Repeat it aloud to yourself several times quickly. To me, at least, the word is oddly beautiful and it is quite strange that it has somehow become associated with a navel. Maybe you're more inclined to the word "c-h-a-n-d-e-l-i-e-r." It has a more sensual toning. **GUIDELINE FOUR: Any time you hear a word that sounds good, stop the class a minute and have students try it out.**

Other qualities inherent in normal, everyday language are rhythm, feeling, meaning, imagination, imagery, etc. I could go on and on. In my experience, the most profitable language qualities to emphasize to children are SOUNDS, IMAGINATION, IMAGERY, AND FEELINGS. As I've said, language and poetry contain many more qualities than these. But this is after all intended as instructional material for teaching children whose language usually is unsophisticated and who have a low boredom threshold. Once children have an appreciation of these poetry fundamentals, they can expand their depth of knowledge.

chapter three

How to Teach Poetry

I think that it is best to start all poetry units with a poetry reading. Students are not going to enjoy the "chore" of writing poetry until they genuinely enjoy poetry in the first place. An entertaining poetry reading is the ideal way to create this sense of fun. When you read poems remember that POETRY IS A PERFORMING ART. Don't just drone the poems, but act them out. Use your voice, make sounds, add expression and feeling. Nothing is more uninspiring than a lifelessly read poem, even if it's one of the greatest poems ever written. If you feel unsure about your ability to effectively read, just remember this bit of wisdom: "CONFIDENCE COMPENSATES FOR ALL INCOMPETENCE." If you haven't the faintest idea what you're doing, just *pretend* that you're confident and students will figure that you must know what you're doing and react to you positively. It might help if you practice before a friend or even a mirror ahead of time. Avoid reading cute, sing-songish poetry.

Poets whose work I've found to be effective to read include:

1. Edward Lear, "The Owl and the Pussycat"
2. Lewis Carroll, "Jabberwocky," and "The Hunting of the Snark"
3. Shel Sylverstein, *Where the Sidewalk Ends*
4. Don Marquis, *Archy and Mehitabel*
5. Ogden Nash
6. Rudyard Kipling, especially his *Barrack Room Ballads*
7. Robert Service
8. Eugene Fields, especially his *Western Verse* about Red Hoss Mountain.
9. *Moon Baby Poems,* by me, David Greenberg. My poetry is about Alligators, Polar Bars, Moon Babies, the constellations, dreams, and many other imaginative subjects.

Now it's time to start writing. But before continuing into several different specific lesson plans for poetry, let me give you some general tips. First of all, a poem need not take any specific form. What you should be looking for in these beginning stages is *poetic use of language,* and it does not matter if it's creatively stanzaed

11

across a page, if it's written in tight grammatical form, or if it's no more than a simple list. **GUIDELINE FIVE: Content, not form, is what counts.** For the purpose of teaching poetry, if a student writes what might typically be called prose, that's OK. Rarely will a student write an entire "conventional poem." What you should be looking for is the image, the sound, the flare of imagination, that sparkle here and there — regardless of the writing form within which you find it. Give a great deal of positive reinforcement, praise, and felicitations when you encounter these poetic sparkles. **GUIDELINE SIX: Only praise — never give negative criticism.** Perhaps you will feel this insincere, but I believe that the beginning stages of writing are so delicate that you want to take no chance of turning a student off — students have so little writing confidence to begin with. What does it matter that a student's first three dozen poems are bad; at least he's still writing with the opportunity of getting better. And if you point out to the students the things you feel s/he's doing right, slowly those things will become predominant. Starting out, at least, you're not expecting to turn out great writers, but simply students who can enjoy poetry.

In presenting lessons, your overall attitude should be whimsical, mischievous, above all energetic. There is definitely a disinterest threshold to be broken. Part of the reason a zany approach is so effective, is that students hardly expect it — they can't believe that their yearly poetry unit isn't sleep-inducing. I think the main reason for its effectiveness, however, is that zaniness is the path of least resistance when children are asked to work their imaginations. It's a safe break from inhibitions especially if you lead the way. Children's imaginations seem so locked away these days, so artificially colored and flavored by TV, that it really is difficult to spark creativity. Mornings seem an ideal time for undertaking poetry, for students' attention spans are generally better then, and your energy level will probably be higher too.

I don't claim all the following lessons are my own. They have been developed with reference to the writings of numerous authors including Philip Lopate, Kenneth Koch, Ron Padgett, and include ideas of my own as well. However, for teachers who are concerned with the practicality of presenting lessons to their class, the material of these other authors is often too diffuse and theoretical. What is presented here is a condensation of these works combined with my own ideas, and is what I believe to be a practical and usable form.

Each of the following lesson plans should be presented in a five stage sequence: A. INTRODUCTION; B. EXAMPLES; C. DISCUSSION; D. WORK-SESSION; and E. PRESENTATION. Let me give a brief explanation of each.

A. In your introduction you should give a short conceptual overview of the lesson at hand. Simply make sure your students have a general idea of the lessons. Introductions usually don't say much and can be boring, so keep the introduction short.

B. Students will really catch the gist of the lesson from examples. **GUIDELINE SEVEN: Always stress that the examples you're presenting were written by other students of the same age** (perhaps an expedient prevarication). The fact that other students who are no older can write poetry gives a giant boost of confidence. With all the following lessons I have provided a number of what I believe to be excellent examples.

Be certain to present a wide spectrum of examples, exemplifying a variety of poetic qualities, for *examples have a very powerful modeling effect.* If you present examples modeling sounds, feelings, imagination, and imagery, you'll get those qualities back in student writing. If, on the other hand, you were only to demonstrate a single poetic quality in your examples, you would get back hardly more than that in student writing.

C. After giving examples it's a good idea to have a discussion to make sure that everyone understands exactly what's happening. Try to build up a friendly competition to see who can think of the most imaginative, amazing examples of their own. Ask for any comments or questions and, according to the lesson at hand, have students start writing on their own or in teams. Just before you have them start writing, however, be certain to remind your students about **GUIDELINE TWO: No Rhyming.** Then discuss **GUIDELINE EIGHT: Tell students not to be concerned with spelling or handwriting.** This makes the lesson a lot less painful and rigid — it helps keep words from getting in the way of

13

poetry. If you don't mention this, you'll probably spend most of your time spelling out words for students. Perhaps at a later point students could recopy their poems with correct spelling and handwriting.

D. Try to give as much personal attention during the work-session as possible. Very often the smallest hint of personal interest can be the greatest writing incentive. I've been amazed in working with students how often the least likely students have had the greatest talent. As a very rough generalization, I have found those students who are most shy and withdrawn and the so-called "troublemaker" students are the best writers, while typical "good" students may not show as much talent. The possible reasons for this are intriguing, but anyway . . . . If you have a limited amount of time or energy, you might consider concentrating it on such unlikely students.

Also, in writing sessions it's helpful if students can have their own personal space where classmates can't easily see what is being written. If you judge your class to be mature enough, have your students spread out anywhere they like in the room to work by themselves or in designated groups.

If a student is really having a difficult time getting anything down on paper, taking personal dictation from him is often a very successful last resort. Or perhaps the poetry assignment just isn't right for a child — in that case urge this student to go off in their own direction — prompt them with other possibilities.

For classes that can't write or have a difficult time writing, there are a number of techniques for eliciting poetry. Again, if you have the time or teacher-power, personal dictation is very successful; perhaps students from upper grades can help. However, it can be just as effective (and sometimes more so) to gather the entire class at your feet and take from them collective dictation on the blackboard. If you want a change of pace from the blackboard, students are very enthusiastic about dictation by typewriter or tape-recorder.

E. When you think adequate writing time has gone by (probably about twenty minutes to half an hour), you should gather all the poems for a presentation. Nothing makes any writer happier or is more reinforcing than to have an audience. **GUIDELINE NINE: It is almost always best if <u>you</u> present student poetry.** This is because students rarely command each other's attention, and you, as a teacher, do; because students have a hard time reading their own handwriting and tend to mumble and speak softly; and because you can edit the poem as you read. Read only the parts of a poem that you like and explain *why* you like some things. With a classload of poems it's hard to make distinctive comments about each, but since this means a lot to students, do your best. Editing also allows you to cut out any possible obscenity in student poetry, without your having to set-up any strict and stultifying guidelines of propriety.

Students may at first be very reluctant to have you read their poems. If you promise them that you won't read names, this reluctance will miraculously disappear. This is most understandable considering the often sensitive nature of their poetry. Another fun way of protecting anonymity is by having your students make up pseudonyms for themselves. Some examples: Pegleg Sam, Sunflower, Rocky, Bugs Bunny, Meatball, The Kid, The Funky Monkey, Blackbeard, Cougar, Beansprout, or the Polish Pumpernickle.

If following your entire poetry unit you were to type up student poems into a magazine (for which students might work out the entire design and production) you would have created the ultimate presentation. If not a magazine, a bulletin board is a fine alternative. Accompanying artwork would go well with this project and would help reinforce the fun of writing.

Guidelines

1. DO NOT ASK STUDENTS TO FIGURE OUT THE DEEP MEANING OF POEMS.

2. WHEN TEACHING POETRY ALWAYS STATE EXPLICITLY THAT YOU DO NOT WANT ANY RHYMING.

3. NEVER FORCE YOUR STUDENTS TO MEMORIZE POETRY.

4. ANY TIME YOU HEAR A WORD THAT SOUNDS GOOD, STOP THE CLASS A MINUTE AND HAVE STUDENTS TRY IT OUT.

5. CONTENT, NOT FORM, IS WHAT COUNTS.

6. ONLY PRAISE — NEVER GIVE NEGATIVE CRITICISM.

7. ALWAYS STRESS THAT THE EXAMPLES YOU'RE PRESENTING WERE WRITTEN BY OTHER STUDENTS OF THE SAME AGE.

8. TELL STUDENTS NOT TO BE CONCERNED WITH SPELLING OR HANDWRITING.

9. IT IS ALMOST ALWAYS BEST IF <u>YOU</u> PRESENT STUDENT POETRY.

chapter four

Lessons

The following may be presented in any order, although whimsical poems are generally more successful starters than "serious" poems.

This preliminary exercise in image-making is good for kindergarten through fourth grade and especially suitable for blackboard dictation.

All you do is make a sound and then ask students what they think it sounds LIKE. Possible sounds you can make include turning a pencil sharpener, pulling a movie screen up and down, screeching chalk, etc. Try to build up a friendly competition in the class to see who can think of the most amazing thing that your example sounds like.

Examples:

Pulling a Movie Screen Up and Down

it sounds like:

rain on a window
teeth chattering
a weathervane turning
typewriter
a rusty door closing
pennies dropping on the sidewalk
keys rattling

skeleton chains
a fish splashing water
applause
toilet flushing
surf
a dishwasher
scraping chair against the floor

File Cabinet Drawer Opening and Closing

it sounds like:

a bell
an engine starting
a choo choo train
waves
a hack saw
a roller-coaster
a washer-dryer
roller-skates
thunder
an ice-scraper
a rake

Pencil Sharpener Sounds

it sounds like:

a can opener
a bed spring
a shopping cart
a train stopping
keys dropping
a bus door opening
dolphin sounds
an egg beater
a snake hiss
a knife being sharpened
a car turning around
a bike skidding

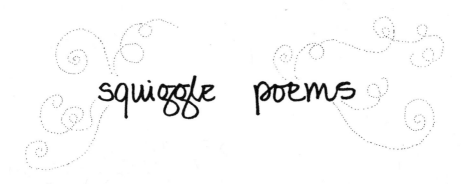

squiggle poems

This is an excellent "starter" poem for kindergarten through fourth grade.

Draw an abstract (and not too complicated) squiggle on the blackboard and have your students dictate to you what, in their wildest imaginations, it looks like. If they're slow getting started, tell them you're really looking for pretend answers.

A variation of this assignment is to have everyone in the class make up their own original squiggle. Distribute those squiggles to your class, directing students to write down, on the same sheet as the squiggle, what it looks like.

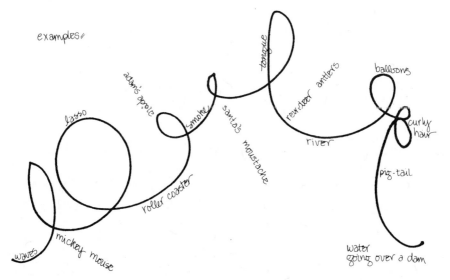

examples:

lasso
adam's apple
smoke
santa's moustache
tongue
reindeer antlers
river
balloons
curly hair
pig-tail
roller coaster
mickey mouse
waves
water going over a dam

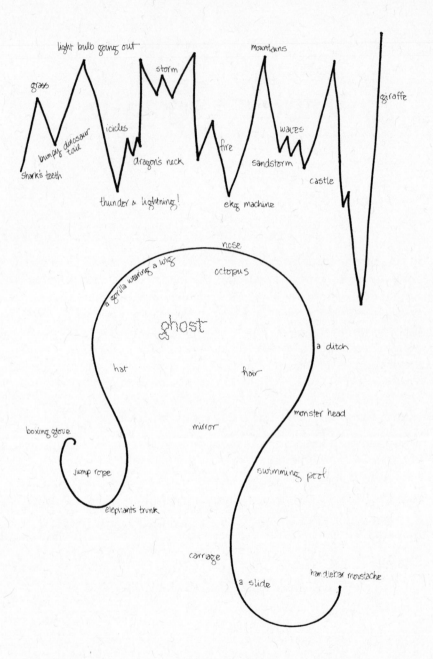

light bulb going out

grass

storm

mountains

giraffe

icicles

bumpy dinosaur tail

dragon's neck

fire

waves

shark's teeth

thunder & lightning!

sandstorm

castle

ekg machine

nose

a gorilla wearing a wig

octopus

ghost

a ditch

hat

hair

monster head

mirror

boxing glove

swimming pool

jump rope

elephant's trunk

carriage

a slide

handlebar moustache

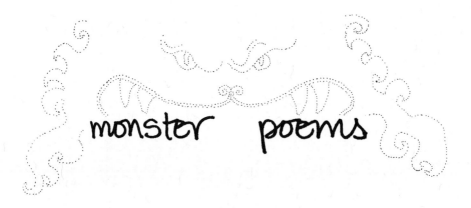

monster poems

This imagination poem is excellent as a very first lesson and perfect for younger students from first grade through fourth grade.

In this poem, students concoct monsters part-by-part. The crazier and weirder this monster can be, the better. Never be content with simple descriptions, always ask for more adjectives describing such things as color and size. In this way students are forced to focus their imagination. Also, this is an excellent poem for students to plug in zany sounds and made-up words. Insist that the description be phrased in terms of simile (i.e. what things are like). You wouldn't want a student to describe a nose as long, warty and green. Get the student to describe it as a pickle. Eyes aren't round, slimy and ugly, but are like raw ostrich eggs.

As a follow-up exercise to this poem, a session in drawing phantasmagoric illustrations is very popular, and I think it reinforces the fun of writing.

If your class is reluctant or unskilled at writing, this is a perfect exercise to do on the blackboard by taking dictation from students.

Examples:

The Killing Krazy Bada-Bada Monster

has:

Sea-horse wrists
Watermelon Chest
Pancake cheeks with mud syrup

rubber pickle chin
fish tail arms
skeleton hands
green bean feet
sword nose
purple potato ears

green banana teeth
grey egg eyes
crazy carrot toes
brown, purple, blue snake hair
stick legs
long orange worm fingers
water hose bellybutton
tire neck

The Galloping Ominous Nose Monster

has:

300 foot bony, purple dragon's tail
a long skinny, scaly-pink-purple-polka
dot neck
With a Zroingy 2,000 eyed face
Long noodle arms
Short stubby 20 twinkle toed feet
Eats deviled eyeballs
Slimy glaring worm eyes that all look
the same way at the same time
Snake fingers
Gooey fingernails as gooey as kidneys
Great big galloppping stomach
And a chopped wormy body
Eats anything in sight

Gooby Dinger

has:

A Dragon head
No teeth
A Worm nose
Apple ears
Yellow tennis shoes
Hairy Ape arms
Pink toothpick hair
2,000,000 green eyes
Orange hot air
Stinger Nails

The Peanut Butter Monster

has:

ten foot long alligator arms
garbage can wings
a peanut-butter bellybutton
axe teeth
ants in his pants
white worm legs
Pink football ears
head: 2 hard-boiled eggs
green polka-dotted mop hair
Color crayon eyes
Carrot spoon toes
Hot-dog fingers on one hand
Fork fingers on the other

dreams

This imagination exercise is superb for first grade and older, and is especially suitable for younger grades when taken in dictation. For older grades this assignment works very well if two to four students collaborate on it — each student writing as much as s/he likes and then handing it to the next student to continue. The idea is to try to imagine what other things or animals would dream of if they really did dream. Asking what their nightmares might be is particularly effective. Be certain, though, that your students maintain originality and don't get hooked into repeating last night's Dracula movie. Again, be sure to elicit as much description as possible.

Examples:

The Lion dreams about a little baby crawling over a log. The baby falls into the river that sounds like there are whales in it. The Lion kills him and eats him.

I dreamed about a moving skeleton. It took me to a box and showed me jewels and gold and money. He took a bag and gave me a whole bunch of it and told me to leave. BUT don't look or he'd kill me. Then he took my stepsister to it and was giving her some gold and jewels and I peeked and it took a knife and tried to kill her. I said I was going to save her, and he said "I told you not to peek." Then I broke all of his bones.

What a monkey
dreams like: A big
bird pulling off
his tail

A rope will be
climbed
The rope falls down
from the tree. The
Indians swinged on
the rope.

I went over a cliff in a car. Trying
to crawl back up. And it
was cold
razor cold
But these creatures whose shape
was no shape at all
wouldn't let me
and I screamed
silently
and told my muscles to crawl
but these creatures pushed me
down through touching me all
over with millions of short fingers
and I screamed
to wake
up

There' were two bad guys wearing black
clothes   my Dad took me for a little
walk at a park in a windy day and we
met these two bad guys and they saw
us coming down the road   they were
hiding behind a tree and they jumped
right at our face   we went to Helen's
house and they got Irish-Setter dog suits
on and when we saw these two dogs my Dad
and I started to pet them and they both
quickly unzipped their suits and
chased us . . . .

frustration poems

This poem is good for first grade and older. The poem is based on a simple formula structure, every line starting with the words "It bugs me when . . .", or "I can't stand it when . . ."

Examples:

It bugs me when I am asleep and I
have to get up. And when it's raining
outside and we have to stay inside the
house. It bugs me when somebody is
in an airplane and I am down on the
ground. It bugs me when a chill
goes up my leg.

I just can't stand it when people
act big on the playground
I can't stand my Dad when he wops
me with his belt!

I just can't stand it when my sister
is at home she really bugs me when
she squirts water through her teeth
at me
I can't stand my dog when at 3 o-clock
in the morning he comes up and starts
licking my face

It bugs me when my sister is in the
bathroom because she gets up at 6

o-clock and stays in the bathroom for an
hour or longer. She closes the door when
she brushes her hair or to brush her
teeth or to clean up the bathroom or
wash her socks in the sink and I get
up at 7:30 and she is still in the
bathroom and I have to go to the
bathroom and every morning I have to
get up to the same thing again. I
go through it again and again and I
CAN'T STAND IT.

I can't stand Lannie's big brother
because he throws me into his 9 foot
deep pool
I can't stand bird stuff dropping
on my head
I can't stand my little brother
because he always says stuff about
me that ain't true

I can't stand being
teased
pushed-around
pestered
called names
ignored
and
betrayed

I can't stand having to go to bed
I can't stand someone scratching their
fingers over the chalkboard
I can't stand someone picking up rocks
with a shovel

It bugs me when
I have to sleep on
the Floor on a cold night.

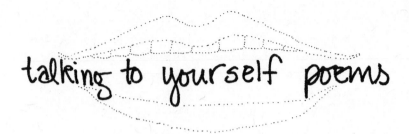

talking to yourself poems

This is another excellent beginning poem, best for advanced second grade and older.

Don't you ever talk to yourself? Don't you ever talk to yourself about all sorts of things, even, sometimes, strange-crazy things? Ask your students these questions — get a discussion going. Then ask them to consider what other people in other walks of life would talk to themselves about. What, for instance, would a fireman talk to himself about? A policeman? A school-bus driver? A teacher? Make sure students are aware of the realistic conditions under which these people work. For instance, a traffic policeman would have to deal with crazy motorists, lousy weather, and exhaust fumes. Wouldn't that affect the sorts of things he would talk to himself about? A fireman on the other hand would be affected by a much different set of conditions and he would probably talk to himself about different things than the policeman.

After discussion, have everyone in the class agree on the sort of person — teacher, fireman, etc. — and write down on a slip of paper a few of the things that person might say to himself.

After the students have finished writing, collect the papers, mix them up, and read them off as a class poem.

The value of this poem is that it forces students to be sensitive, to step outside themselves, and to consider the thoughts of another person. It also demonstrates that poems need not follow a logical or rational sequence of thought.

Examples:

Bus Driver Talking to Himself

Those little Pigs! I hate those brats.
Man, they think they're so cool. I
wish that they would put their foot
in their mouth and munch. "Shut-up
you kids before I stop at the slaughter-
house and have you slaughtered!!"
"Quit honking my horn before I toss you
into the street!" STOP SHOOTING SPIT-
WADS!!! I wish I could fill their mouths
with quickdrying cement and dump them
into the Columbia River. I wanna get
fired. OH MY GOD! President Carter
could do better. I'd rather be in a
crocodiles mouth. I QUIT!!! I'm going
to scream. U-U-U-U-U-U-G!!!!! I
wonder if these kids ever get tired of
themselves? This isn't a bus full of kids,
it's a ZOO.

Old Lady on Bus

Oh dear, I forgot where I'm supposed to
get off at. Henry, how are you doing
down there? Is it hot like they say?
You young whipper-snapper!
Why do these young kids always have to
push and shove? I'm not as fast as they
think I am. I wish I was young again.
Oh those kids; the things they do these
days! And the girls are something else —
the way they dress, let cigs hang out of
their mouths. I just don't know about
it anymore.
Boy when I was young I would have
never
talked back to my mother!
Stupid kids, all they care about is

31

themselves.!
I've got to go shopping next week.
Here I am shopping in Lloyd Center and
it's 8 AM
I wish I didn't wakeup!
I can remember when I was young. Yes,
those were the good old days. How I
loved my jean shirt and halter tops.
Now I don't know which is worse, my
arthritis, stretch marks, wrinkles, or
bum ankle.
Yes, those were the good old days.
I wish I had a maid.
I wonder if it is time for school.
I wonder if I paid when I got on this bus,
or did I?
My arthritis is bugging me again.
Where am I supposed to get off this bus?

Teacher

Ding! Ding! Ding! Ding! OH
DEAR I have to get up every morning
to go to work. Darn this stupid
car it never starts. Finally got
to school.   OH DEAR this classroom
is a mess. Jim! SIT DOWN! Stop
cussing and curb your tongue Tony!
We are going to do spelling now.
Hey you sit down. Ding! Ding!
Ding! Ding! Ding! It's lunchtime.
Lunch over. These kids always fight.
OK time to do math. Ding! SCHOOL'S
OUT!!

like poems

This poem is good for blackboard dictation, but is also excellent as a first written poem for advanced second grade and older. This is actually a lesson in the power of simile though it is taught here at an intuitive rather than a mechanical level. Here students learn how to articulate images by comparing them to something else.

As a second stage of this assignment, or as an entire separate assignment, you can pay attention to "synesthesia." Synesthesia is expressing a sound as a smell, an object as a sound — or in other words, intertwining the senses.

Other possible variations of this assignment include taking one object and seeing how many different similes can be created around it. Or, students can be asked to consider different textures of emotion they have felt and then be asked to decribe these emotional states through simile.

Examples:

> *A water fountain is like a cobra*
> *The full moon is like a pearl*
> *Spaghetti is like boiled worms*
> *A swamp is like a slug*
> *A bald head is like a hard-boiled egg*
>
> *A plate is like a flying saucer*
> *My Mom is like a lion*
> *My dog is like a mudpuddle*
> *A football is like an eye*
> *The alphabet is like a long word*
> *Snow is like popcorn*
> *A pair of scissors is like a bird*

A swing-set is like an old tree blowing
in the wind
Dancers are like water . . . .

A tree is like a pinecone
A blackberry is like a superball
A clock is like a face looking at you

A stapler is like an alligator
A skyscraper is like a giant with billions
of eyes
A bubble is like a space-ship
A wet beach is like the crust of a pumpkin
pie

The back of a teacher's chair looks like
a jail
The grill on the front of a car is like
a 4-eyed kid wearing braces
A telephone pole looks like a beef jerky
stick
Your nose looks like two endless tunnels.

The rain is like little men jumping
on your roof . . . .

Hair is like:

spaghetti
worms
mud
an oil slick
hay
yarn
a mop
a clothes brush

a porcupine's back
pig's tail
telephone cords
SLIME
fuzzy shower mold

The rain falls
in the Falltime
like falling stars
The snow falls
in the Wintertime
like cream

A pear is like:

An upsidedown balloon
a hand-grenade
a lightbulb
a FAT lady
a keyhole
An eight
A bear swallowing a rat
a snake head
a skull
a guitar case

synesthesia:

A Tiger is like Thunder
The smell of incense is like sad music
a feather pillow is like a breeze
A train whistle is like Dawn
The sun is like a red-hot
A whisper is like a cloud
Sunset is like death

emotions:

My sadness is like an old pair of
shoes gathering dust—holes in their
soles, no laces

A Foster kid is like a pinball machine,
getting bounced back and forth

The years that go by so fast are like

    Moths

The time I came home from summer
camp I felt happy . . . like a dolphin
leaping out of ocean. But also at
the same time I was scared of the
new year . . . like the way a frightened
rabbit shivers when you hold it . . . .

Sometimes I feel like a robot, rusted
Other times, I am unhappy, like an
animal being killed . . . .

As happy as circus clowns with funny noses
As sad as raindrops covering my face like tears
As mad as fire burning the house
As angry as a rubber-band shooting
As scared as a broken down old house with
bats
As brave as a man fighting a shark

may poems

This is an excellent poem for a beginning group, advanced second grade and older, because a great deal of structure is provided simply by directing students to start each line of their poem with the word "May." They then fill in the rest of the line with the most outrageously imaginative thing they can think of. It is the purpose of this lesson to get students to stretch their imaginations — to think in terms of absurdity, exaggeration, zaniness, or in other words, the ludicrous.

If a student has a hard time getting started with this assignment it often helps if you suggest a very specific situation. For instance, suggest that the student imagine sitting in class during an arithmetic lesson; then ask what would be the weirdest, most impossible thing that could happen.

Another helpful incentive is to make this into a lying competition. Tell students that all you want is the biggest, fattest lies they can think of.

Crazy, made-up words fit well into this sort of poetry.

Examples:

> *May one morning, instead of putting*
> *toothpaste on my toothbrush, I accidentally*
> *use ketchup instead*
> *May an alligator wear lipstick*
> *May Smokey the Bear smoke cigarettes*
> *May apes wear fur coats*
> *May you be kissed by a green slimy oozy*
> *hunk of rotten fish head*

May a green and purple striped Tyrannosaurus
Rex walk into this room right now and
tapdance on my nose.
May a bee make peanut-butter and jelly
May a near-sighted Boy Scout kiss Godzilla
on the nose
May Wolfman sing love songs
May a volcano sprout flowers
May the principal swing from the lamps
like Tarzan
May an oogle-doogle do a boogle on my
noogle

May a dog walk on its ears
May the sun turn into ice
May snow turn into comets

May an Imba-Bimba Kookamaonga monster
swallow the Empire State Building . . . . . .
and then BURP and destroy the world!!!!

May your face turn green and your nose
fall off . . . May slime cover your face,
and your ears wrap around your head,
and your eyes be on your big toes.

May the moon stand on a rainbow
May the streetlights jump up and down
May a fish ride a horse
May the world turn inside-out

May your brain walk out of your mouth
May a desk fly away
May a green and blue cow play basketball
May a warthog wear panties

Illustrations are, again, a good accompaniment to this exercise.

alone poems

This poem, best for third grade and older, very powerfully explores students' feelings. It will help students to look into themselves and then to articulate their feelings, incorporating their image skills from previous lessons. Starting with this one general, yet identifiable, feeling in themselves, children will be on the path to further introspection and articulation so essential to poetry. The poem simply works by starting each line with the word "Alone." Students can draw from their own experience or they can construct evocative images. Stress that you want *complete* descriptions.

Examples:

> *Alone is going to bed at 3:15 in the morning*
> *and getting up at 7:00 in the evening with the*
> *wind blowing*
> *and leaves flying all over*
> *the place*
>
> *Alone is out at recess by yourself when*
> *everyone else is playing together*
> *Alone is the minute you turn your back*
> *people start talking about you*
> *Alone is when you know all the questions*
> *except one, and that's the one the teacher*
> *asks you*
> *Alone is on your horse in the middle of*
> *the desert*
> *Alone is a ship in the middle of the ocean*
> *just like a single Willow tree in an oak-*
> *forest*

Alone is in the middle of the night
when you have to go to the bathroom
Alone is when you wake up after a night-
mare
Alone is dying and being in a coffin alone

Alone is when you're in a fight and
everyone else is on the other kid's side
Alone is when you move to a different
neighborhood and you don't know anyone
Alone is playing tennis by yourself
Alone is when you come home from camp
and nobody asks you any questions about it

Alone is fishing in a river all by yourself
Alone is eating by a campfire on a cold
night when the owls are awake
Alone is living in the woods by yourself
Alone is laying on a grassy sunny hill
looking at the big blue sky, watching the
birds fly by
Alone is sleeping in the sleeping bag out
in the dry backyard looking at the crystal
white stars in the dark black sky
Alone is sitting under a green shady tree
eating your lunch by yourself
Alone is a yard with no grass

Alone is your Mom and Dad fighting

Alone is like a clock with a
missing number
Alone is like a basketball team with one
player
Alone is like a flag with no pole
Alone is like a knob with no door
Alone is a desk with nothing in it

Alone is a baby at night

Alone is when you move into a big new
house with your own bedroom
Alone is a dog at night-time in the dark
Alone is the book left in the library
after moving day
Alone is the lost slipper you've been
looking for
Alone is the new car you were about to buy

Alone is when you try to say you're
sorry and they don't accept

Alone is slipping under the covers and
feeling the cool sheets

Alone is dressing by yourself in the
locker-room
Alone is eating bananas
Alone is after you get in trouble
Alone is when you're embarrassed
Alone is having no one to talk to
Alone is being sick and nobody comes
to visit you

Alone at a party. . . . Oh there's so many
people, but still I feel all alone, just
sitting there and thinking

Alone
is
when
you
don't
have
any
friends

Your students will probably feel a lot less inhibited about this
poem if you suggest they use pseudonyms.

formula poems

This kind of poem works for advanced third grade or older. Several lessons already presented have been based on simple formulas (e.g. starting every line with the word "May" or "Alone"). Formulas are a very successful "poetry starter" because the student doesn't become sidetracked into form. The student can concentrate entirely on the far more important poetic content. Here are some examples of other successful formulas you might try.

Examples:

Nothing . . . .

Nothing is an old empty house
Nothing is a thought that can't be told
Nothing is the number of pages before
chapter one
Nothing is the drive down to Mexico before
you get there
Nothing is trying to follow a fishing line
through the rocks
Nothing is running your hand over your
forehead before you reach your hair
Nothing is the gallop of a horse, for it
goes on and on and on

And Nothing is reality next to imaginary

A Monster . . . .

A MONSTER is your mother when she
is about to spank you for doing bad
A MONSTER is what the kid down the
street looks like after you beat him up
A MONSTER is the blind date your friend

picks for you on a Saturday night
A MONSTER is your brother's girlfriend
A MONSTER is what your mask looks like
and your friends don't believe you're
wearing one
A MONSTER is either you or me

Being Surprised . . . .

Being SURPRISED is when you know something neat and everybody else knows it too
Being SURPRISED is finding out that your
blind date really is blind
Being SURPRISED is when you are caught
necking with a girl in your class
Being SURPRISED is when your friend says
he found one million dollars and you
don't believe him. The next day he comes
to school in a chauffeured Cadillac wearing
diamond rings.

Suspension is . . . .

SUSPENSION is getting in a fight
chewing gum when you're not supposed to
not sitting down when you're told to
talking about the librarian and how old she is
hitting the teacher
getting up late in the morning
doing your artwork
cooking breakfast by yourself
watching afternoon television: Perry Mason
watching soap-operas with my mother
going to pay bills with my mother
staying home and babysitting my niece
watching other people come home from school
getting back in school the next day

Happiness is . . . .

Happiness is going home for the first day
of vacation
Happiness is Friday
Happiness is holding your pet
Happiness is doing something with your family
Happiness is getting something new
Happiness is giving
Happiness is finding a ten dollar bill

Boring is . . . .

Boring is school
Boring is taking out the garbage
Boring is having to clean your bedroom
Boring is having to go to bed early
Boring is doing work
Boring is going to music
Boring is having to stay at the baby sitter's
Boring is having to walk to school with
your sister

Friendship is . . . .

Friendship is meeting someone like you
Friendship is being able to talk to someone
Friendship is telling secrets
Friendship is walking home with someone
Friendship is someone that will bring you
up when you are down
Friendship is having someone over to spend
a night

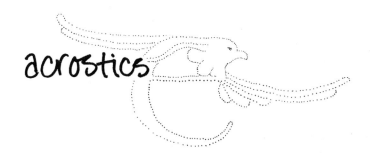

acrostics

These are imagination poems for advanced third grade and older which put a strong focus on vocabulary. Students choose any word (perhaps their own name), line it up vertically on their paper, and start the first word of each line of their poem with the letter on that line. If students can't think of words, this is an excellent excuse to get them to use a dictionary. If they get to a spot where no word seems to fit, maybe a sound or made-up word will work.

Examples:

      Elephants step on them
      Giraffes gulp them
      Geese lay them
    I Scramble them

      First day of school
      Inside we walked
      Viewing the walls
      Everyone gasped

      One boy even fainted
      All of us laughed
      Kicking with puzzledness
      Submarine sandwiches were all over the walls!

      Bubble bath bumble bees
      Eat yellow jacks for breakfast
      And chew ACROSTICS for lunch
    and Nutritious noses for dinner
        Yuk!

Live long my friend
Ah shall you too
Undo the wrong string and you may not
Rong again!
Ashes fall

So much nonsense
Twas when did we start to fight?
Ehhh I don't know
Pretending.
Pretending.

Poets love potatoes
One poet fell in love with a sweet potato
Today they were pronounced Mr. & Mrs. Greenberg
At the ceremony they got in a fight
Tomorrow David Greenberg is to go on trial for
        Mashing a sweet potato
his Only hope is to break out
Except he won't
his Sentence will be two years peeling potatoes!

Noodles and oodles of noodles
    Oh how I love oodles and oodles of noodles
        Oooops they slid down on the floor
        Darn! I missed you my darling
    Love them, so much. . . . they slide down your
        throat
EmmmmmmmmmmmmmmmNOODLES!
Swimming and wiggling in your stomach. . . . .

Sam chewed a slug sandwich
    However they came out of his nose
    One crawled back up his nose
    "Eat some more" said Mother

Come on, try it.
Open your heart
Unusually kindhearted
Right now, do something nice
All the time you're scared
Gee! have some courage
Everyone should have a little bit of courage

riddle poems

This poem is best for advanced third grade or older students. It works best when two or three students collaborate, alternating between questions and answers. This is an exercise in the use of imagination which appeals to children's love of riddles. In one sense this is actually an exercise in mythic imagination, for aren't myths simply imaginative, unscientific answers to unusual questions?

Riddles are principally of three types: How did certain things come to be? What are certain things made of? How do certain things work? Students will write a greater range of poetry if you make a point of explicitly stating these three categories.

A variation of this poem is to have students make up "impossible" riddles on separate slips of paper, mix up those questions, and distribute them to the class for answers.

Examples:

> *What's in the stomach of Jaws?*
>> *Food stamps, license plates, United*
>> *States flags torn up in pieces, and*
>> *Webster's dictionaries*

> *Where was monster Zero born?*
>> *At the island of Mysterious Things*
>> *like scalped people, and puny little*
>> *psychedelic Dinosaurs.*

> *What's in the center of the earth?*
>> *Cinderella's glass slipper*

What makes a person lonely on a deserted
beach?
      The Sound of Wind and Love

What is the ocean?
      A restaurant for fish

What is a dinosaur?
      An overgrown salamander

How does a shark make a living?
      He executes fish

How does King Kong scare people?
      By his bad breath

What does an alligator play?
      He plays snap-jacks

How come Adam & Eve ate the apple?
      Because they were hungry

Why are cops called Pigs?
      Because they don't take no hogwash

Why do ducks quack?
      Because they ate too many noodles

What do alligators eat for breakfast?
      Zoo-keepers

How come they don't send mice to the moon?
      Because it's made of cheese

How do you know you're not living in a
dream?
      Because red anteaters don't eat pickles!

Why do stars fall?
> They're glued onto a black piece of
> paper . . . when the glue dries they fall

What's the Milky Way made up of?
> A Milky Way candy bar

Why do birds fly?
> It's too far to walk

Why is King Kong so big?
> He eats bananas

Why does it rain?
> Because the ground is thirsty

Why is Mars red?
> Because Earth kissed Mars

How come boats float?
> If they sank we wouldn't have them

How come noses are so long?
> If they were short you couldn't fit your
> finger in them

How come you have toes?
> So you can lick the toe-jam out of
> them.

recipe poems

Here is a poem, good for fourth grade and older students, that can really unleash some of your students' more "extreme" creativity. This poem is not necessarily good before lunch — though on the other hand, maybe gastric juices enhance creativity! The whole idea of this poem is to make up creative recipes for real or imaginary dishes. Write the recipes down in the same general form found in genuine recipe-books.

Examples:

Slug Soup

Bring to boil pot of stagnant water. Then take 6 cups live slugs in large mixing bowl and beat with egg-beater, add worm juice, octopus eyes, and mold off inside of garbage can that hasn't been cleaned for at least a year. Slowly add to water. Boil down to a fine ooze, sprinkle with fingernail clippings. Serve

Roast Platypus

Catch Platypus
Shave off whiskers
Remove tennis sneakers
Hang upsidedown for week in clothes closet
Coat in tinfoil, sunglasses, and suntan lotion
Place in 350° oven for 3 hours,
or until well tanned
Send to Miami Beach Florida with one way ticket

School Lunch

First take all students who are late with their homework assignments, chop finely, add dash of onion, garlic, oregano, and simmer on low heat. Then add chewed up bubblegum scraped off bottoms of desks, pencil shavings, and 4 quarts of Elmers glue. Add raw teacher brains, principal toes, and fish guts. Roll into hot-dog shape. Serve on buns with mustard and relish.

Gut Stew

Slimy squid guts + dinosaur eyeballs + live spiders. Boil down until lumpy. Add toejam + alligator tongues + live frogs. Place in volcano and bake until crust forms on top. Take neighbors pet + aardvark liver + spices, blend smooth in blender, and mix with other ingredients. YECCCCCCCCCHHHHHH!!!

Atomic Pie

Crust: Mix sawdust with hippopotamus fat, dash of garlic, and ammonia flavoring. Roll out.

Filling: Fill pot with dirty socks, limburger cheese, moldy apricots, and hairy peaches. Bring to boil. Then throw ingredients out. Finely grind up pot and let sit for two years. Add to crust. Bake. KABOOOOOOOM! CRUNCH! UGGGGH! You have just created an atomic pie!!!

facade poem

This lesson seems to work best with fourth graders and older students. The lesson will focus on the difference between the way students seem to be and the way they really are. In other words, it will explore children's "own little world." This lesson is not only valuable because it gives children an awareness of who they are inside, but it also allows them the realization that all people — even the most confident, seemingly popular people — have inner worlds. This assignment can be worked with the formula "I seem to be . . ." "But really I am. . . ." Or, if your students have had enough writing practice, they can break away from this structure and simply write free-form about "their own little world."

Students can either write directly from their own experience or they can experiment with figurative images. Again, pseudonyms are a good idea with this assignment.

Examples:

> *I seem to be a dancing clown*
> *But really I am a burning tree*
> *I seem to be a sun shining bright*
> *But really I am a dull rainy day*
> *I seem to be a swing swinging high*
> *But really I am a lonely cat*
> *I seem to be a laughing joy*
> *But really I am a crying lost girl*

I seem to be happy
But really I am sad
I seem to be wanting my own world
But really I am not wanting my own
> I do not want my own world because
> it would be so hard to manage. And
> it would be too big for me. And I
> would be too small for it.

I am sitting in my House
sinking deeper into myself
I can feel myself starting to raise
out of my body. I feel just
like two eyes. It feels so good as
I say to myself I begin to float
as if I were on a cloud. I say to myself
I can fly like an eagle
I can soar in the sky
I feel like a cloud drifting
slowly. I can go slow or
I can go fast I like to
go slow and see everything and
feel the freedom. As I come
back to my house and drift
into myself I say I was
free I actually soared through
the sky.

as I say this to
myself that's my world

Freedom
is my world!

I'm alone in my special world
I like my world,
I like the peace,
I see the flowers,
The sea and sky,
I walk along wooded trails
I watch the animals and birds
I love my world
Just me, the stars, the sun, and
my very own world.

I seem to be a person who tries to
make people laugh
But really I am a person with terrible
jokes
I seem to be a person who smiles a lot
But really I am a lonely person who
keeps things to myself

My sister says "I'm out of it"
My brother says "I'm always laughing"

But in my inside I'm
dreaming of owning a horse
and what I'd do if I got one.
I'd feel proud and happy. I'd ride
it down the beach and make
it gallop into the sunset and
we'd walk all night in the Black
lonely world till the sunrise peeked
up over the mountain then we'd
run all the way home and
all the way I'd say

"home girl"
"home girl"

mannerism poems

(A poetry game). Appropriate for fourth grade and older, these are not so much conventional poems as they are exercises in observation, an ability so essential to the poet. It really is not physical characteristics which make a person unique, but his minute behavior, his posture, habit, manner, or way of talking. In this exercise students spread out around the classroom and spy on one another to detect these mannerisms. They can also recollect one another's mannerisms. Be certain to stress that mannerisms are particular habits one person has *that hardly anybody else has.* Stress that mannerisms *are not* physical characteristics, they *are not* common habits.

After the writing session, the mannerisms for a specific fellow student are read aloud without revealing his name. Other students have to guess the identity of the student just from the list of mannerisms. This exercise can be hilarious, especially when students find out about their own mannerisms.

Many teachers are often apprehensive that students may become malicious or derogatory in writing their mannerism lists. I find this to be very rare, especially if you start the lesson by providing examples of positive (maybe even affectionately teasing) mannerisms.

Examples:

> *cracking knuckles*
> *chewing on fingernails*
> *tapping pen on desk*
> *tilting back in chair*
> *playing with hair*

eating hair
sitting on desks
Always says "Baby! Baby! Baby!"
Always says "Oh yeah!"
Always playing with buttons on shirt
Walks with hands behind their back
Wiggles their nose when thinking
Hums tune to Star Wars day in, day out
Always pretending they're driving a car

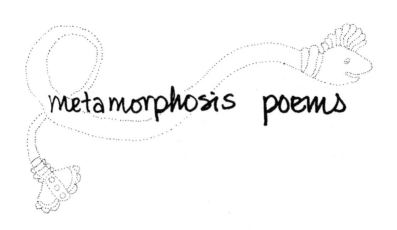

metamorphosis poems

This poem works best with fourth graders or older. It directs students' attention to things that can be the same, yet different. It's based on the formula "I used to be . . .", "But now I am. . . ." It is very important that everyone understand this "same yet different" concept, so discussion should be emphasized.

Examples:

> *I used to be a beautiful whispering oak tree*
> *Now I'm an old Brown book that's never read*
> *I used to be a big red Drum*
> *Now I'm an addition to the dirty city dump*
> *I used to be a sickly pink Baby*
> *Now I'm a full grown Boxer*
> *I used to be a huge white cloud*
> *But now I'm just a drop in the gutter*
> *I used to be a baby mouse*
> *But now I'm the thing that the cat*
> *brought home.*
>
> *I used to be a big mean bear*
> *But now my head hangs on your wall*
> *I used to be a big fierce alligator*
> *But now I am your wallet*

I used to be a baby red Robin, but now
I'm a mother Robin
I used to be grass, but now I'm a
bird's nest
I used to be a blue lake, but now I'm
a splashing ocean
I used to be a silk worm, but now I'm
a piece of silk

I used to be a hunk of iron
But now I am an old hammer, banging
my head against an anvil

I used to be a young apple tree
But now I'm a dream that never came true

I used to be an 8 ft. spud
but now I am 9 boxes of potato chips
nobody buys
I used to be a polka-dotted pig
but now I am an oval thing that gets
thrown around
I used to be a cow
But now I am somebody's size 15
leather converse

I used to be a pig that nobody liked
But now I am liked by everyone since
they cut me into bacon

I used to be a forest with a meadow and
stream
> *But I'm now an airport for jumbos and*
> *people who really don't take time*
> *to feel Beauty*
I used to be a rabbit soft and sheer
> *But now I'm a lucky token for a person*
> *that's not*

I used to be a little
BRAT
But now I am a bigger
BRAT

I used to be a dinosaur,
Now I am what makes your lawnmower go

myth poems

This poem, best for advanced fourth grade and older, can be very beautiful. Take an animal, plant, or natural phenomenon and express it in an evocative manner. Start by discussing how different things have different qualities which make them unique. For instance, a horse has speed, it has color, it has a certain smell, it can be gentle in a certain way, and wild in a certain way. A cheetah or a kangaroo, on the other hand, have different kinds of speed, color, power, gentleness, wildness, physical characteristics or habits. Once you have started distinguishing unique qualities, describe them evocatively — often using similes. Writing in the first-person adds a powerful mythical texture to this poem.

Examples:

> *I am the bald eagle*
> *My beak is as sharp*
> *as a golden eagle*
> *My wings can spread as far*
> *as the sky*
> *My eyes sparkle*
> *I am the eagle*
>
> *I am the rainbow*
> *I am as colorful as a tulip*
> *My blue is as light as rain*
> *My red is as bright as a rose*
> *My green is as bright as the grass*
> *My violet is as a daisy*
> *My pink is as a blanket*

I am Jaws
I can swim as fast
as a cheetah can run
My teeth are as sharp
as the longest sword
I love to eat people
I can control thunder

I am the sunflower
I am as bright as a piece of gold
I make people as happy as a clown
I am as tall as an eleven foot tree
I am the sunflower
I look like a hand
waving in the breeze
I am as pretty as a rose
I am the sunflower
I make people bright and happy

I am the Fighting Eagle
strong, fierce and wild
My beak is like a strong fish hook.
My claws are like a dozen nails
or a dozen sharp knives
I am the Fighting Eagle
faster than the wind
stronger than ten elephants
I am the Fighting Eagle
My wings are bigger
than the tallest giraffe
I am the Fighting Eagle
When I eat, the world is peaceful
When I sleep, the whole world sleeps.

I am the Thunder Horse
My neigh is like thunder
That's how I got my name the Thunder Horse
I run faster than the wind
My gallop sounds like a herd of buffalo
I am the Thunder Horse
When lightning hits me
where ever I am, good things happen

I am the black cat that slithers and slides
I am a good hunter at night
I go hunting for mice
I am the cat
that comes home in the morning
and eats my breakfast
I am the cat
that takes my nap
I am the cat
that's as black as night
I am the cat that purrs when you pet me
I can catch mice as good as a trap
I am as fierce as a lion that's mad.

I am the volcano
who lives on a hill
I am as loud as the biggest thunder storm
I am stronger than 1000 Bulls

mit
translation poems

This poem works best with advanced fourth grade and older. It is a difficult lesson and only students or classes who have shown writing aptitude are likely to be successful with it. An arbitrarily chosen poem in some foreign language is written on the blackboard and read aloud. Students are then asked to give a creative translation — to write down what they think it means. You must stress that their translation must hold a continuity from line to line. They should not try to translate each word independently. If they can't translate a word or line, they should simply make up anything they like or skip it altogether. Or they can go off entirely in their own direction. It helps if you suggest that the poem should hold an overall storyline.

This is an excellent assignment for attuning students' ears to sounds, for most of their translation will be based on sound association.

To prepare your class for this lesson, here are some sample lines in French which you might like to try reading aloud.

     a. *Il y a une pamplemousse dans le closet.*
Could mean: There's a purple moose in my closet.
           Who put the pantyhose in the skillet?

     b. *Je suis fous a la tete.*
Could mean: I flew in a jet
           You're a fool I bet

     c. *Ou est le tricot?*
Could mean: Who ate the tricycle?
           You're staying in the treehouse?

Examples:

"Hälfte Des Lebens" (a German poem)

Mit gelben Birnen hänget
Und voll mit wilden Rosen
Das Land in den See
Ihr holden Schwäne
Und trunken von Küssen
Tunkt ihr das Haupt
Ins heilignüchterne Wasser

Weh mir, wo nehm ich, wenn
Es Winter ist, die Blumen, and wo
Den Sonnenschein
Und Schatten der Erde?
Die Mauern stehn
Sprachlos and kalt, im Winde
Klirren die Fahnen.

translations:

Snoopy was walking down the street
one day he saw a rose
and he suddenly fell in Love he
said to the rose what nice golden
petals and what tasty wine. . . then
they both saw a drunken man
and gave him her wine then the
rose said that is my cousin
then Snoopy said you better leave
or I will beat your face in
then Snoopy found out the man was
Andy the Alligator

Crunch. . . . . . . Snoopy and the rose are
gone

A monster ate a ball
and a mint wooden rose
Dad landed in the sea
He ate Dad too

I had a scarecrow
And trouble came fast
He took my scarecrow too
With the help of a walrus
We managed to cook him
Ow Oh Eeeeck
That grease hurts me
He finally was done
And we ate him

This goblin burped hot dogs
And vomited wild roses
The land was naked
1 hour late he did it again
And tumbled on it
And wiped it on his rump
His mother helped him wash up
Oh. . . . Mother I'm going to do it again
OH NO
Muhammed Ali
Help me please?
Let me be a champ like you
Oh No now I'm letting gas
Fight me Muhammed!

Meet Gelben Birman my pet,
and also meet Weirdo Rose,
and in the dead sea they live.
1 year in shame, and trouble, in
prison, tucked and stumped, in
the stealing business were they.
They met Wilber the ugly.
A few weeks later Weirdo Rose
died. To make a long poem short
they lived happily ever after. . . . . .

A French Poem by Apollinaire

Ton sourire m'attire comme
    Pourrait m'attirer une fleur
Photographie tu es le champignon brun
       De la forêt
      Qu'est sa beauté
      Les blancs y sont
      Un clair de lune
    Dans un jardin pacifique
Plein d'eaux vives et de jardiniers endiablés
Photographie tu es la fumée de l'ardeur
      Qu'est sa beauté
      Et il y a en toi
        Photographie
    Des tons alanguis
      on y entend
      Une mélopée
Photographie tu es l'ombre
      Du soleil
Qu'est sa beauté

translations:

*Ten sour mattresses are coming
Mattresses are stuffed with sour
flour. Champion photographers are
delivering them by the seconds.
They deliver them in the forest
They are so beautiful.
They sing songs so well. They're
favorite tune is Clementine.
They swim in the Jordon Pacific
Ocean. The mattresses are always
on the river with little kids on
top. Some photographers are so
small they have to use ladders
to get on top of them. They have
lots of beauty. I tell you they do.
Yes tons of mattresses are coming
in. Everybody loves them.*

A ton of marines are coming
One of them wants to fly
Photographs are one's desire
One likes forts
One questions beauty
One balances beads on Sundays
One makes chairs
One guards the Pacific
One steals janitors valuables
One studies fumes in a larder
Bugle blowing's for one
One shouts when he eats
One collects portfolios
One does acrobatics
One paints entrance signs
One makes teepees
One ruins lumber
No soul dares
To question these marines

photograph poems

This is another advanced poem assignment best for fifth grade or older. In a way, this is a continuation of the "Mannerism" poem — the object being to precisely capture the essense of an experience. In any experience there are certain details which make it stand out. Such details should be accurately recorded in this poem.

Examples:

> *Riding on the bus and*
> *Sitting by the window*
> *feeling very squished and*
> *very uncomfortable and*
> *I am very tired, then*
> *all I'm watching is the*
> *bus driver. He takes his*
> *hand off the wheel and*
> *sticks his hand down*
> *his shirt and pulls out a*
> *watch and the whole*
> *bus laughs then I*
> *looked out the window*
> *and felt the wind whipping*
> *against the window*
> *as if it were going to*
> *cave-in.*

In the grocery store

The grocery store was very busy
*   like bees making honey in*
*   the springtime*
In the back of the grocery store,
*   a woman stuck a pair of extra*
*   size panty hose up her shirt*
The bakery section smelt like
*   burnt apple pie*
The grocery store on that hot
*   summer day smelt like a*
*   bad case of foot fungus*
The kind of music that grocery
*   stores play reminds me of a*
*   cow's funeral.*

In the Airplane

*   I felt like my stomach was*
five feet above my head
*   When we took off, my parents*
said to look down and enjoy the sights,
*   The clouds looked like big*
fluffy marshmallows.
*   We passed the clouds and then*
saw the ocean so far below.

I was on a bus and got
stuck between some big people
They were talking over me
and I could not help from
hearing what they were saying.
I got a feeling that I was
being pushed around it sounded
like they were talking about me
being so small and I got the
feeling that they didn't like me being
so small Finally
they got off the bus I felt
like someone was going to start a fight
with me

Being in the car for six hours and we got out only once

I felt squished
I got a headache from being bored
Since I had a headache, I couldn't
read or write
I ripped at my hair

My hair slipped through my fingers
like wet spaghetti noodles from
perspiration
My head felt like my brain was beating
like my heart
My heart was beating 560 miles an hour
My face was green (at least it felt
that way)

It reminds me of throwing a temper-tantrum.

Portland

Green, Green, it's good to be back
Green, Green, Where is the city? The Houses?
Ah! There it is!
Green, Green, Home sweet Home
There's the House!
Look at the grass!
Green, Green, Home sweet Home

the darkness of the night
the quietness of the house
no light in the house
the open window
no one in the house
the dogs barking outside
the cat playing with marbles on
the tile floor and then
jumping at you
the feeling of someone watching
you
the people talking outside
the monster movie on television

then comes the knock at the door

fictionary

(A poetry game). This is an hilarious imagination game, good for advanced fifth grade and older, that makes using a dictionary fun. Simply divide the class into groups of four to eight. One person in each group leafs through a dictionary to find some outlandish word for which everyone agrees they do not know the meaning. The person who finds the word writes down the real definition on a slip of paper. Everyone else in the group then proceeds to creatively fabricate their own definitions for the word and will write it down on slips of paper. The person who found the real definition then collects all the definitions, mixes them up with the real definition and reads them all aloud. Group members then vote for whatever definition they think is the real one. If an individual votes for the correct definition they get a point; if someone has their definition voted for, they get a point. Group members take turns looking up words.

Examples: (Can you guess the correct definitions? — answers at the end of the lesson.)

I. Branks:
    a. a bamboo warbler used for decoying ducks
    b. Scottish tavern game similar to shuffleboard, but smaller and using leather push discs
    c. a metal clamp for holding a woman's tongue in place
    d. imprinting device used in the manufacture of shoe soles
    e. organ used instead of kidneys in most birds

II. Galantine:
   a. a boned, stuffed, jellied bird
   b. flagship of 18th and 19th century English fleets
   c. engineering term: uniformly sectionable bridge span
   d. condition arising when viscous igneous matter cools along a vertical rill
   e. a mating moose

III. Lemur:
   a. a skewed integument
   b. mucal lining of inner skull
   c. nocturnal, jumping monkey
   d. female leper
   e. any of several North American plants (genus Lemuriana) with dark-blue, closed, tubular flowers, blooming in the fall

IV. Daut:
   a. a navigational caliper
   b. fernicular cloud movement, associated with descending high pressure systems
   c. to correctly punctuate a sentence
   d. archaic: date (as in date tree)
   e. to fondle

V. Leptodactylous:
   a. chronic epidermoid erosion
   b. Latin term for Alligator
   c. psoriasis of the armpits
   d. having slender toes
   e. the ability to leap with one's fingers, as with Lemurs

Answers to Lesson 20: Ic, IIa, IIIc, IVe, Vd.

I wish you luck in presenting these lessons. If the results you get don't seem spectacular at first, remember that the examples I've provided here are some of the best from thousands of students — most people simply are not great writers. If your students enjoyed the assignment, then you've accomplished a great deal.

73

Bibliography

I have found these books useful in teaching poetry to children.

Koch, Kenneth. *Rose, Where Did You Get That Red?* New York: Vintage Books, 1974.

Koch, Kenneth. *Wishes, Lies, and Dreams.* New York: Vintage Books, 1970.

Lopate, Phillip. *Being With Children.* New York: Bantam Books, 1976.

The Whole Word Catalogue. New York: Virgil Books, 1972.

"Teachers and Writers Magazine," Teachers & Writers Collaborative, Inc., 186 West 4th Street, NYC, NY 10014.

Poetry to read aloud and poetry children enjoy reading:

Carroll, Lewis. "Jabberwocky," and "The Hunting of the Snark."

Fields, Eugene. *Western Verse.*

Kipling, Rudyard. *Barracks Room Ballads.*

Lear, Edward. "The Owl and the Pussycat."

Marquis, Don. *Archy and Mehitabel.*

Nash, Ogden.

Service, Robert.

Sylverstein, Shel. *Where the Sidewalk Ends.*

Greenberg, David. *Moon Baby Poems.* My poetry is about alligators, polar bars, moon babies, the constellations, dreams.